INTERDEPENDENCY

Interdependency

How to Reform the Criminal Justice System. A View From a Criminal Defense Attorney.

MARIA D. CICCONE-FIORENTINO

Jonathan M. Fiorentino

REDBABY PUBLISHING

Redbaby Publishing, Inc.

INTERDEPENDENCY:
How to reform the criminal justice system. A view from a
criminal defense attorney.

Maria D. Ciccone-Fiorentino

REDBABY PUBLISHING

ISBN 978952163111 eBook.
ISBN 978952163128 Paperback.

Dedication

This book is dedicated first to my husband, Frank, who has given me the encouragement and faith to put my thoughts about prison reform on paper; also, to my son, Jonathan, who used his creative skills to bring about my views of reform, and my son Nick and his wife Brittney, who both supported and encouraged me throughout the writing of this book. Also, I thank TJ, who has been of great assistance in finding the right words to bring across my ideas while I was writing this book. And to all my friends and neighbors who have been anxiously awaiting the publishing of my book and wish me every success in bringing my thoughts of reform to the people who may bring about true and lasting change to the system.

And above all I thank God almighty who instilled in me the intense passion for criminal justice, the compassion to represent all my clients in their cases to the best of my ability, and His still small voice that has gently nudged me with the urgent need to write about the necessity to have compassion and even respect for the offender in order to reform the criminal justice system. Without all this, my book would not have become a reality.

Introduction

For decades, there have been frequent conversations but paltry attempts at altering our criminal justice system structure. As an attorney representing inmates in post-conviction relief, I have been a witness to the structures' many obstacles, vulnerabilities, and deficiencies. As an attorney representing prisoners on their petition, I am not an authority in all the facets of criminal law reform. By writing this publication, I will point out those obstacles and viable solutions. Reforming the policy is not a straightforward undertaking. My stand is that my reflections and theories may yield some shifts in the minds of the authorities in order to rebuild the system in a fashion that has perhaps never been considered. The criminal law system comprises six parts, each with its own function: law enforcement, the bail system, sentencing statutes and processes, penitentiaries, and parole/probation. Police have been enforcing the law in America since colonial days, but do they protect and serve each community without bias? By peering into its past, we can understand that some elements have strengthened while others have continued the same. The recent clamor for "defunding" the police has created intentions for police reform, but its purpose must produce fresh understanding, direction, and genuine change. This is where police reform must happen.

The bond system still calls for considerable reform to shed the imbalances between the rich and the destitute, people of color and white. The fewer individuals who are awaiting their trials in incarceration, the less capital is being allocated by the system to keep them housed. It can then circulate this wealth for more constructive purposes. Keeping defendants in custody before their trial only leads to more dilemmas, such as loss of employment, economic hardship, family, medical, and psychological issues.

The latest advancement in revising sentences has been the legalization of marijuana in some states. Some laws have legalized a specific amount, while other laws have not changed, convicting simple possession of marijuana for up to ten years or more depending on whether the offense was a first, second, or third charge. The one large change has been the use of marijuana or its ingredients for medicinal purposes. Despite these changes, the laws for possession and distribution of other drugs such as cocaine, crack, heroin and other narcotics still remain illegal. Maryland has eliminated the mandatory minimums and double sentences for drug crimes that have contributed to mass incarceration. It is this mass incarceration that has introduced the greatest need for reform. Vested community partners and legislators need to re-examine sentencing guidelines to determine if they are not only fair, but also serve the purpose of each individual offender in their rehabilitation. The word "rehabilitation" should replace the word "reformation" because rehabilitation means restoring a person back to the position he was originally in prior to the offense. In actuality, the offender finds himself back in the same negative environment that produced his criminal behavior, initially. However, when an offender becomes reformed by the use of an individualized sentence and innovative and beneficial programs, it becomes a more positive and favorable situation which would cause a more productive and law-abiding life.

Prison reform has been a subject of major debate and discussion for many years. The elimination of mass incarceration should be the principal goal in prison reform. There are far too many people languishing in prison without receiving proper rehabilitation, adequate mental health services, drug and alcohol treatment, and necessary medical aid. Reforming the sentence structure would be a part of prison reform because each inmate would receive an individualized sentence geared towards specific factors, along with an individualized reformation program. A primary issue in prison reform is the treatment of inmates by the prison authority and staff. There have been many horrific stories written about the inhumane treatment of inmates both in the federal system and in the states. The solution is establishing stringent hiring standards that properly vet all prejudices, biases, and violent tendencies, along with higher educational requirements. I value this as one of the most important issues because the proper treatment of inmates with respect, dignity, kindness, understanding, and tolerance affects the performance of the inmate as he progresses through his program. As the old saying goes, "you catch more flies with honey than you would with vinegar."

The last part of the system is parole. Many parolees have expressed to me their fear of being returned to prison based upon a minor violation that is not even a crime. This happens more times than I can count, but this is only part of the problem. Basically, parolees are working within a broken system which has failed to benefit them for many decades. The system is riddled with racial disparities that lack transparency. Hearings that take months if not years to complete, be little, if any help to parolees in acclimating themselves back to society in such a way that they become productive and law-abiding members. In Maryland just recently, the Legislature has voted to remove the governor from the parole decision for lifers after they overrode the Governor's veto on the bill. Having the governor involved in this decision was more political, and even former Governor Glendenning has testified that this was a mistake on his part. The parole commission possesses a great deal of power so that it is unnecessary to involve the governor in the decision-making process. It is for this purpose that we must address parole reform. For what is its purpose? Is the purpose to lie in wait; we should reform a parolee to violate parole or revise agencies and services that aid the parolee to become a better person? We must pursue the latter in order to decrease the recidivism rate and be a part of ending mass incarceration.

Finally, in the last chapter, I will discuss the issues of corruption, oversight, racism, and community reform. Corruption has existed in the system for decades but nevertheless I feel we must address it with oversight as its solution. It is sad to say that Maryland leads the nation in racial disparity, 70% of the prison population is black, and blacks serve longer terms whether by conviction through a trial or pleading guilty with the expectation of a lesser sentence. Only two of my clients are white. Finding the solution to racism is difficult, but it must begin in each person's heart. I firmly believe God has created us all and hatred towards any race different from one's own should not exist. Can you imagine what the world would be like if racism and its disparities did not exist? As John Lennon wrote, "Imagine all the people living life in peace. You may think I'm a dreamer, but I'm not the only one." Didn't Dr. King talk about having a dream? It is this dream we must all strive to attain. Oversight should begin with the police from the moment they arrest a person, up and then throughout the parole term. Only through oversight will we possibly prevent corruption, errors, prejudices, illegality, and any other issues that produce unfair practices throughout the system. History has documented that poor black/brown neighborhood have higher crime rates, and it is these neighborhoods that need reforming and uplifting. To reform only the criminal justice system will not address the root of crime. If we can eliminate even a small percentage of crime from these neighborhoods, it could have a positive effect on the reformation of the entire system.

Last, and more important, parts of the criminal justice system: the police, bail, sentences, prisons, and parole require reforming so they are interdependent upon one another. The purpose of each part should be the common goal of reforming and not just rehabilitating the offender. For if each part of the criminal justice system works in unison with each other, only then will we achieve a true and complete reform that can decrease recidivism and end costly mass incarceration. Today, many people talk about reforming the police, bail, prisons, or parole separately, but this results only in a piecemeal reform. Reforming all the parts of the system together and simultaneously will produce a criminal justice system that can operate in unison for one common goal. The reform of all these parts will cause the availability of funds needed to make those changes. Mass incarceration, constructing more jails, lengthy prison terms for misdemeanors, felonies and all drug crimes, only results in a very costly system that cannot transform the offender into law-abiding citizen. The gold thread that should weave throughout the system should be one of respect, dignity, and love, no matter what race, creed, sex, or age. As you go through each chapter, I derived the recommendations I have formed from my personal and expert reflections, research, and personal interviews. I realize also that these recommendations may come with a high price tag. However, by substantially reducing mass incarceration by the elimination of all drug crimes, lengthy sentences, reforming the bail system and other vehicles, those funds would then be available for more beneficial purposes that would reform the system.

Even though some of my recommendations are "radical", I hope they will at least spark great debate to think out of the box and maybe produce the reform that is so direly needed for such a long time. With all the current events that have taken place and the great division in our country, I only hope and pray that we as Americans can show affectionate acceptance for each other's differences, respect for the rule of law, kind treatment of one another no matter the differences, and the strong desire to become better people who can make this country the way our forefathers intended and to make it that shinning city on the hill.

Chapter One

The Police

In order to reform the police, we must first understand why policing began and how it developed in early American history. The history of the police dates back to the American colonies. The purpose differed from the North and South, where some parts were to control new immigrants while other parts were to control slaves. During the colonial days, the police, known as "night watch" comprising criminals who observed and protected communities as a form of punishment. As one may suspect, the "night watch" failed to perform as expected. However, in the South, the police known as the "slave patrol" was to capture escaped slaves and lasted until the Civil War. After the War ended, immigrants from Germany and Ireland flooded the Country. The "night watch" found their methods to keep order ineffective. This marked the beginning of a police force and became established in almost every major city to prevent crime and keep order. It wasn't until the 1900s that a new police force came into being. [1]

Even though this is only a very brief accounting of its history, one can see that we have made minimal changes since the beginning. The black and brown population is still being harassed and persecuted and killed either by gunshot or some type of brutal strangle hold. The question to ask is, does the past purpose of the police meet our present needs? A resounding "no" is the answer. Our needs today are far different, but unfortunately, only the outer appearance of the police force has changed. Since the brutal murder of George Floyd, the outcry has been to "defund" the police. The word "defunding" means to take away funds, but to do this would ignore the present needs of our communities. As a community, how can we reform the police to better fit our present day? We must look at improving and building stronger communities that have high crime rates. The issues to be addressed are the safety of the inhabitants, improving the schools in those communities, providing for better employment opportunities through the establishment of agencies to provide job skills, and the availability of social services, medical and mental health services, and drug/alcohol treatment within those communities. It is from these needs that we can reform the police. I will say more in the later chapter on community improvement.

Reforming the police to meet the present-day needs involves a re-inventing, a restructuring, and a re-defining of the police's new purpose. Reduced funding is not the answer. A redirection or allocation, along with additional funding, is necessary to meet these needs. In the beginning, the police, considered "peace officers," and their purpose was to keep the peace in their assigned areas and neighborhoods. I recall in my early years that small business owners and the officers that "walked their beat" knew each other on first name basis. In residential areas, they knew the police as helpers in times of need. Unfortunately, the negative attitude and treatment of blacks in poor neighborhoods changed little from the colonial days. This is clear in the death of George Floyd and others that came before and after him. They must resurrect and expand aid to the communities. Hiring standards must improve in order that the character, personality, and personal beliefs become just as important as basic qualifications. Today, most police departments require a college degree to be considered for employment. I believe that qualified candidates should have course work in social work, criminal justice, or psychology with ongoing requirements of post degree studies. Candidates with foreign language skills should continue. Even though police departments perform extensive background checks prior to hiring, emphasis should be on vetting for any violent tendencies, biases, and prejudices towards any race, creed, or sex. Extensive testing and interviewing of a candidate should be the norm, for the police force should comprise professional people with a superior knowledge and understanding of the communities, residents, and business owners and the problems they face. They need to be compassionate people with a great desire to help those in need. With the resurgence of white supremacists and the many extremist groups both on the left and right, it is vitally important that these extreme views be prevented from infiltrating the police, but also removed from the police force at all costs. Investigations into police behavior and views once hired should be a continuous procedure to avoid the development and infiltration of these extremist groups into the police force. As Pat Robertson, a well- known evangelist, recently stated, we need to hire the best and brightest people because training is not enough. It is "who" the police departments hire that makes the difference. Then training instills the professionalism and further knowledge needed.

The training of the chosen candidates also requires improvement and change in order that the officers can meet the present needs of their designated neighborhoods. Basic training needs to be expanded to include the ability to de-escalate possible violent situations along with the ability to access what type of situation is occurring quickly. Legislation should eliminate choke holds, no-knock warrants, knee to neck, and other dangerous procedures and substitute with other more humane procedures that will de-escalate violence and result in a more peaceful outcome if an arrest is warranted. More in-depth training on what specific circumstances should be used to avoid injury and death of an unarmed suspect. The firing of a gun should be one of last resort or for self-defense. They should perform arrests and interrogations with extensive knowledge and training of the law and legal procedures in order that there is a lower risk of a violation of rights. Just as in other professions continue educational courses and training should be provided in order that officers are current on the latest techniques and legal issues that affect their profession and the neighborhoods they patrol. Police departments comprise many units such as narcotics, homicide, vice, and swat teams. What is needed today is the inclusion of social workers, mental health professionals, and mediators who would belong to an unarmed unit to work with armed units when necessary. Such professionals would have basic police training geared towards their purposes so that they could aid the suspect and the armed units either with mental health issues, crisis negotiations, drug and alcohol addiction, and domestic violence. They would also have the duty to assist officers in dealing with the pressures that are associated with the police profession. In San Francisco, California, they created a behavioral crisis intervention unit made up of social workers, psychologists, and other professionals who are not police officers. They patrol the streets in marked vehicles depicting their crisis unit, unarmed, and respond to non-violent situations. They even assist homeless people in crisis by referring them to other agencies to find housing and other help they may need. If a situation should turn violent, they bring in the police for support, but continue to stay involved in resolving the situation. The unit, funded by business tax, has taken the police out of crisis situations that rarely result in arrests or violence of any kind and situations where poorly trained police have very little knowledge of how to manage these situations. These crisis intervention units should become a new form of policing and considered by other jurisdictions and states. We should use Swat Teams only for intense hostage and terrorist situations and not for routine felonies and misdemeanors. Police dispatch will have the duty to access or triage a situation based on the information given to them by the officers on the scene and their needs for those situations. The latest situation the police are facing today are all the hate crimes perpetrated upon various races, such as assaults against the Asian and Jewish people. Police would receive training and continued educational courses to understand and learn proper methods and procedures to manage and de-escalate these situations so that they result in a positive outcome. I recommend holding regular town hall meetings with police, social workers, and mental health professionals to aid and guide the residences and business owners to understand the nature of hate crimes and other problems that arise and find possible peaceful solutions.

Recently in Maryland, the Senate Judicial Proceedings Committee passed the last of a package of Police Reform Bills, making it the first state to do so and overriding Governor Hogan's vetoes. It provided that the failure of an officer to activate his body camera created a rebuttable presumption that the testimony of the officer is inadmissible in a criminal prosecution. We can discover much evidence through the use of these cameras and their de-activation will only lead to an abuse of power and only be de-activated during off-duty hours. In addition, I recommend daily inspection and testing of body cameras to insure proper operation if they are not already being performed by present practices. We must train officers in de-escalation procedures and implement a system is to identify officers who are at risk of using excessive force. Records relating to an investigation of police misconduct are not to be considered as a personnel record according to certain provisions of The Public Information Act. There must be complete transparency concerning all police conduct. Without it, there will be no accountability for wrongful and illegal actions by the police. Using excessive force was also addressed by prohibiting an officer from the intentional use of such force and also requires officers to use force only if it is necessary and proportional. It also made it a requirement for another officer to intervene to prevent an officer from using such force and to report to a superior officer regarding such actions immediately. Another bill required no-knock warrants to be approved by both a supervisor and the state's attorney and be between 8 am and 7 pm, barring exigent circumstances. Another bill established the Task Force on Independent Investigations Involving Deaths Caused by Law Enforcement Officers. With passage of these bills, more states are moving towards police reform, especially holding individual officers accountable if their conduct amounts to any violation, whether legally or ethically. On the federal side, there are police reform bills that still await passage, but the major obstacle is qualified immunity. We judicially created this type of immunity many years ago that shields government officials from being held personally liable for constitutional violations such as the right to be free from the use of excessive force for money damages. It would be beneficial to have federal police reform legislation along with the individual state police reform laws. The reform in this area should hold police officers liable both civil and criminal for such use. In civil actions, the state, county, or city liable will be held liable for those actions. The state, county, or city government would pay the money damages along with payment from the officer by a reasonable attachment of liens or other methods. The defense to holding officers liable is recruitment. Federal and state authorities feel if police were to be held liable, it would be difficult to recruit people to join the police force.

However, with all that I have advocated, by hiring the best and brightest people along with the stringent hiring and vetting processes and continued surveillance, those hired would not have the inclination to use such force unless absolutely necessary and within the parameters of the law. In order to hold police criminally liable, we must establish laws outlining what actions are criminal with all the elements needed to prove such criminal actions. Unfortunately, the federal bill named the George Floyd Policing Acing passed the House of Representatives, but not the Senate. Negotiations are in process, but it is difficult to predict whether the bill will pass in its present form, changed in order to agree with both Democrats and Republicans, or not pass at all. However, many states are creating and passing their own police reform legislation. In my final chapter, I will discuss the use of oversight throughout all the parts of the system as an independent third-party committee and racism, corruption, and community improvement.

The most important aspect of police reform is how the police interact with their assigned communities. We cannot ignore the basic purpose of the police to keep order. However, their visibility and actions in those communities should be at the forefront of reform. In middle class neighborhoods, and in more affluent areas, we view the police as aides in times of crisis. However, poor black/brown neighborhoods view the police are an agency only to harass, brutally treat, and in the worst situations kill the residents who may be unarmed. This is pure evidence of racism that must be eradicated at all costs because reforming the communities and the system will never be a success until racism no longer exists and is no longer tolerated by society. Along with the improvement of high crime communities, officers' training will be geared towards the specific community they are assigned to protect. This results in the creation and development of trust and the officers will have extensive knowledge and training to be an aid to those communities instead of a force that only harasses, brutally treats, and arrest the inhabitants. The police are the first encounter for offenders in the criminal justice system. Therefore, police reform should aim at setting up an offender for success and not failure as he proceeds through the system. One purpose of integrating police into specific neighborhoods is that they form a bond with the residents with the goal of aiding and improving the lives in those neighborhoods. The police would work with the different agencies, such as drug/alcohol treatment, mental and medical health, job skills and employment agencies, and improved schools within those neighborhoods. Police and community leaders should hold periodic town hall meetings in the communities they work along with the residents and business owners to keep abreast of the needs and problems as they arise. New legislation that has passed in the recent year and after the conviction of Chauvin is proof, that society and politicians are more than aware that police reform is outdated and requires a massive overhaul. These new laws are headed in the right direction. Unfortunately, establishing rules and procedures that the police must follow is not enough for one is asking an "old school" officer to abide by new rules. What also needs to happen is the re-defining of the police, their role in society and their communities, and the creation of a new officer who understands the needs and problems in those neighborhoods with the superior knowledge of how to engage with the residents to foster trust and together find solutions that will improve lives in those communities. Each part of the system must work together in unison and be interdependent upon one another so that it results in the reformation of an offender to a law-abiding citizen and the elimination of mass incarceration.

1. The Insider, Protests Against Police Have Broken Out Across the Country. Here's how Policing has evolved in

the US since its beginnings in the 1600's, by Frank Olito, 6/2/20.

Chapter Two

Bail

The bail system in Maryland is very simple. It works by releasing a defendant prior to his trial in exchange for a certain amount of money. The court holds that money until the defendant's trial is completed. Afterwards, the money is returned to the defendant. The money is a guarantee to assure that the defendant will return for his trial date. Specifically, there are two types of bail: the cash bail and the surety bond or bail bond. The cash bail is usually a set amount (or scheduled) for misdemeanors and non-violent crimes. Bail bond is for felonies that incur a higher sum. Family or friends of the defendant will go to a bail bondsman, where they put down ten percent of the bail along with some type of collateral. The procedure begins with the defendant appearing before a court commissioner within approximately 24 hours after arrest. The commissioner reads to the defendant the charges and penalties, his right to an attorney, right to a public defender if he cannot afford a private attorney, and determines either the amount of bail or if they can release the defendant on his own recognizance. If they do not release the defendant, he then will proceed to his bail hearing. The defense puts forth evidence to advocate other alternatives to bail instead of being kept in detention or released on bail prior to trial.

Unfortunately, this present system works against the poor and black/brown population. Many people languish in detention centers prior to trial simply because they could not afford their bail amount. In February 2017, Maryland adopted new laws that would allow judges to release defendants who had unreasonably high bail amounts. This reform only made matters worse. Even though they released more defendants, judges ordered more defendants to be held without bail or a much higher bail which they could not afford for fear that those defendants would commit more crimes if released. In the end, it only left the same number of defendants sitting in detention centers. The problem with this reform is that it failed to provide judges with alternatives which is where reform should start. In most felony cases, a request is made for a risk assessment to determine if the defendant poses a flight risk and is done prior to the setting of the bail amount. Risk assessment involves looking at the defendant's prior crimes, if he or she was present at all court dates, a review of psychological and medical evaluations along with drug/alcohol screening, employment record, family information, and financial data. The purpose of this in-depth evaluation is to determine what avenue would be best for the defendant as an alternative to detention and bail that he or she could not afford. The only reason they would detain a defendant prior to trial is that he or she would be a high flight risk, the seriousness of the charge, and for public safety. Other defendants charged with lesser non-violent crimes are released into an individualized community-based program called a "bail program." This would eliminate the need for cash bail. This program aids the defendant in confronting various issues and to assure a higher probability that he/she would return for the court date. Based on the risk assessment, the defendant may be required to take part in drug/alcohol treatment. If necessary, the courts will recommend and/or provide any medical or mental health treatment, or take part in psychological counseling depending on the nature of the crime charged, and any diagnosis made. This bail program will allow the defendant to avoid loss of employment, financial hardship, and family issues since they would release him, while providing the help he needs to resolve addictions, mental health, and other issues that may have caused his criminal behavior. The bail program would be akin to a type of supervised probationary period prior to trial. A bail program report would be submitted to the court, defense, and state that would show any progress and/or any further assistance that would be necessary. If they found the defendant not guilty, then based upon the bail program report, he could continue in the program until completed as an assurance that the problems uncovered in the report may be resolved. This, in turn, would lower the possibility of the defendant being involved in criminal activity in the future. If found guilty, the bail program report would be used as part of the PSI (pre-sentencing investigation). This bail reform would then tie into the sentencing reform so that all the parts of the system worked in unison. During the sentencing phase, as discussed in the next chapter, the court, from the PSI and bail report, along with expert testimony, would have all the information needed to make an informed decision as to the type of sentence to render. By reducing the amount of people in detention awaiting their trial, it would create or free-up money that would be used for the bail program. This then would reduce the recidivism rate by providing the help defendants need to overcome their issues and would increase the defendants' chance of returning to court on their court date because of the supervisory nature of the program.

Chapter Three

Sentencing

It seems as if the entire purpose of sentencing a defendant to a term in prison is one of punishment, and rightly so. However, what must be considered is how much punishment should an inmate experience. The basic punishment is that we remove a person from his place of residence, his family, friends, and his freedom to live his life is taken away. Unfortunately, the punishment goes far deeper. We can say that punishment is like the rearing of children, but what is the result when a child is continuously punished, but never rewarded for exemplary behavior or given the opportunity to strive for a right way of living? We have found that this overly punitive rearing only leads to negative results. As previously mentioned, one gets more flies with honey than with vinegar. Inmates are poorly treated by prison authority and staff; medical and mental healthcare is lacking, as well as drug and alcohol treatment. Educational and vocational classes are only for those with minor sentences and, if available to all the prison population, there is a long waiting list to be accepted. If there are no jobs available within the prison, most of a prisoner's time is spent in his cell. It is not unusual for an inmate to take a class or course more than once simply because he has taken all that he could take. It is also rare that an inmate, once released, can claim that he has been totally reformed so that he is adequately prepared to live a law-abiding life and no longer engaged in further criminal activity. Most are released with only fifty dollars and the few possessions they have accumulated during their prison term if they desire to keep them. Most can say that we have not trained them in any type of vocational skills that will support them on the outside, for the system cannot provide such job skill programs within the prisons. Basically, they are put back into society in the same position they were in prior to their arrest, only to face the same negative environment that led them to criminal behavior in the first place. As previously mentioned, reformation of the inmate should be the goal, not rehabilitation, for reformation will place the person in a more favorable position than prior to his arrest in order that he may be a success on the outside and to avoid falling back into a life of crime. The goal of sentencing is the manner in which an inmate is rehabilitated or as previously stated "reformed." The present notion of punishment should be removed and instead the need to assist and support an inmate to become a better person should be the norm. When looking at the juvenile justice system, the goal is to keep the juvenile out of the criminal justice system and to aid them with the various problems they face. The goal is to prevent them from becoming career criminals. This goal should be the same for the adult population in the sense that it will reform them to become better people, taking them out of a criminal life style and with desires and opportunities to live a normal and prosperous life. For I firmly believe that all humans want to live a good, healthy, and law-abiding life, but unfortunately many lack the opportunities that are available to a more affluent class of people. The Declaration of Independence reads, "We hold these truths to be self-evident, that all men are created equal, that they are endowed by their Creator with certain unalienable rights, that among these are life, liberty and the pursuit of happiness." In reforming sentences, these truths that our Declaration speaks about must guide us and provide those opportunities whereby an offender can achieve these goals.

After we pronounce a defendant guilty either by judge or jury or pleading guilty, the next hearing would be his/her sentencing hearing. Prior to that hearing, a PSI (pre-sentencing investigation) is conducted which involves a detailed evaluation of the defendant, which should entail psychological, psychiatric, mental, medical, prior criminal record, employment history, family, and financial information. This would also include the bail report, as explained in the second chapter. A PSI hearing should be held in order that testimony from these reports be given by experts with their recommendations as to an individualized reformation program. The major change that should be made is the elimination of life and long-term sentences. Several non-profit organizations have advocated that these sentences cannot produce positive outcomes, but only further the suffering experienced by prisoners, and continue mass incarceration. In the end, it only changes the prisons into "nursing homes" for offenders. An examination into all the categories of crimes must be performed to determine not only the length of a sentence but also the reformation program that each inmate would receive. Already "second look" policies have been enacted in 25 states to review long sentences and reforms have been made throughout the country. Washington, D.C. recently passed the Second Look Amendment Act to expand release opportunities to people who were convicted under the age of 25. Because of this new Act, 29 percent of the prison population will be eligible for re-sentencing. Also, in New York, a second look policy was created to look into the elderly prison population. Even The Sentencing Project, a non-profit organization based in Washington, D.C. who is a leader in changing the way Americans think about crime and punishment, is recommending that states and the federal government review inmates' sentences after they have served 10 years. Many people in prison, after a certain age, pose a minor threat to public safety, but have no hope of being released, much less any chance of an opportunity to achieve a productive law-abiding life on the outside. The second look policies and reforms recognize that these long sentences are unjust and even inhumane and that there are better alternative methods to ensure public safety. Those methods would encompass the reforms and programs I am advocating. The goal is to change the offender and improve their changes so that a criminal life style is no longer desired and a positive productive life is attainable.

All drug crimes, whether possession or distribution, should be irradiated for addiction, is a disease, not a crime. We may consider the elimination of all drug crimes radical, but who are these crimes harming? The harm is to the actual user, however, that is the choice they make, and one can say that the seller is praying upon the user to make money or to support their own habit. However, these crimes are not morally wrong and are not to be included with more serious crimes, such as murder and rape. There, the harm is instantaneous and for life. With the elimination of all drug crimes comes the reduction of mass incarceration. When mass incarceration is reduced, it increases the money to fund drug and alcohol treatment programs and other programs because the system is not spending funds to house drug offenders. The problem to be solved is, what happens to the manufacture and sale of all these illegal drugs once taken off the books? Just as the farming and sale of marijuana has become a regulated business, the same should occur with other narcotics. Through regulation and licensing, the production and sale would incur taxation, and that could create drug treatment programs not only in high-crime neighborhoods and schools, as previously discussed, but also within the prisons.

Through regulating the manufacture of narcotics, we will regulate the strength or potency of the drugs. It is ironic that the money that could be derived from the taxation of the drug industry, could be the money we would use to decrease drug usage. We must accept the fact that drugs will always exist in our society. However, we must re-direct our efforts into decreasing drug addiction by treating it as a disease instead of treating it as a crime. Sentencing the user and seller to long prison terms only increases mass incarceration, and suffering, and the prisons that cannot provide the drug user with the addiction treatment he needs. Decreasing drug use can only be done by providing the incentive to do so through innovative and intensive drug treatment programs, whether within the neighborhoods or inside the prisons. Many of the violent crimes may be caused by drug use, but if we institute the proper drug programs within certain neighborhoods, schools, and prisons, those violent crimes may be reduced. Also, drunk driving laws include driving under the influence of drugs, and these laws should remain the same.

Today, courts disseminate life and long-term sentences like candy on Halloween night. This practice must end except under certain circumstances because it only serves to continue mass incarceration and cannot assist the inmate to better himself by providing no hope for a future outside of the prison walls. Even life sentences without the possibility of parole should be only under rare circumstances. We have also documented that many prisons are becoming nursing homes because of the aging prison population. This change must begin at the sentencing hearing when the judge determines what type of sentence and program is warranted for the individual offender. To decide, the judge relies on the outcome of the PSI hearing, the bail report, and the PSI, along with any testimony

necessary. Judges would be trained in all the different reformation programs available in all the surrounding prisons and
will even be able to rely on testimony from the experts man-
aging those programs and whether it will suit the offender for
a specific program. This is very similar to what happens in the
juvenile justice system, where a program is found for the juvenile through testimony of psychologists and social workers
who are knowledgeable about those programs. The sentence
to be handed down would be based upon all these resources,
would be an individualized program only geared towards a particular offender and his needs, and would be for an indeterminate term for more serious felonies and some definite terms for
lesser felonies and misdemeanors. By doing this, the notion of
punishment would be removed and replaced with the idea of
reformation and support. More importantly, once in a program,
the offender would be constantly monitored and evaluated for
any progress or failures. Programs would be comprised of drug/
alcohol treatment, such as the 12-step program, mental and
medical health treatment, psychological and psychiatric counseling and treatment, as well as vocational and educational
programs.

The offender would not be considered for parole until he
has successfully completed his program, met all its requirements, and has been psychologically tested for any possible issues that would hinder his release and success on the outside.
This can be akin to attending college with all the scholastic requirements and a goal of a level of excellent achievement. Having indeterminate terms for more serious offenses may also
seem radical because such an offender may be released only
after serving a short period. The possibility of this occurring
will be built into the system by the length, difficulty, and requirements of each program. For these offenders indeterminate sentences would be necessary because one must take
into consideration the difficulties, failures, repetition of failed

sentences, and psychological counseling and testing to avoid "working the system" by the offender not to mention completion of drug/alcohol treatment, vocational and educational programs. If the sentences were for a specific term, there could be the possibility that the offender would not have completed his program as required by the end of his term.

Recently, there has been discussion concerning the elimination of life sentences without parole and capping those sentences by 20 years or another specific amount. However, this does not take into consideration the nature of the programs discussed above. The program is similar to a college major in a specific field of study that makes up the changes in the sentences to be rendered.

When considering the sentence, a judge must also decide if the offender is one who can be reformed by the program or one who is not reformable due to either unresolved psychological issues, risk to public safety, being repeat offenders, or lack of remorse. Again, the judge relies on the offender's PSI, bail report, past record, victim impact statement, his risk to public safety, lack of remorse, and testimonies of the experts who conducted the offender's evaluation with their conclusion whether the offender can be reformed. It is only when an offender is not able to be reformed that he would receive a life sentence. That life sentence would still give the offender an opportunity to better himself and change the direction of his life if he were able to meet stringent requirements and a high degree of success. There would still be continuous monitoring and evaluations to measure his progress, along with psychological counseling, to discover any concealed criminal notions on the part of the offender. Despite all this, there are cases where the offender is unable to improve and continues to demonstrate violent tendencies and an ongoing criminal state of mind. It is in these cases that a life sentence would continue until any positive changes occur in the future or as an offender approaches an elderly age.

Another form of sentence would be an alternative to prison. This form of sentence would be for minor crimes, misdemeanors, and non-violent offenses. There are diversion programs in Maryland, however, these are for offenders who have served a certain amount of time in prison or who are about to be released. By diverting these low-level offenders away from prison and into a diversion program, mass incarceration would be further decreased. Also, these offenders would not be housed with the more serious offenders who might have an influence on them and their behavior. These programs would either be in an in-house community-based facility or on an out-patient basis and would involve drug/alcohol treatment, medical and mental healthcare, educational, and vocational training including development of job skills and employment assistance, and community service. The judge would determine at the sentencing hearing which diversion program would be appropriate for the offender based upon his PSI and other reports and testimonies previously mentioned, or whether the offender should be put into a prison program for a certain term or until successful completion. As with the other programs, the offender would be constantly monitored and evaluated to determine his progress or failure. Release from any of the programs would be decided by the parole commission upon successful completion of the program. Parole reform will be discussed in the later chapter of this book.

Recently, much has been handed down from both federal courts and various state courts concerning whether juveniles should be given life sentences without the possibility of parole. In the case of Graham v. Florida, the Supreme Court went into a detailed discussion of the immaturity of juveniles and that to sentence a juvenile to a life sentence without the possibility of parole would not take into consideration his maturity over the years and would provide that juvenile with the realistic opportunity to obtain release after those years have passed. Several other state courts have ruled similarly, however, even to impose a life sentence with the possibility of parole to a juvenile would only add to mass incarceration. Life sentences, whether for an adult or a juvenile, should be given in only very limited circumstances where there is no show of remorse, a risk to public safety, repeated violent offenses, and where an offender repeatedly fails to complete his program successfully.

Another new bill has been passed by the Maryland Legislature dealing with juvenile life sentences. This bill prohibits life without parole for juveniles and allows those offenders, who were tried as adults and had served at least 20 years, to have their convictions reassessed. This new law is going in the right direction, but I feel it needs further improvement and reform.

As can be seen from the beginning, that when an offender is exposed to the system, the purpose of aiding the offender instead of punishing him is the goal. Community improvement by having drug/alcohol programs within the communities and providing better schools along with agencies for the development of job skills and employment assistance will also have a great impact on criminal justice reform.

The involvement of the police in the neighborhoods they patrol is one of directing the possible offender into programs that will aid them to better themselves and their life situation. However, once arrested, the bail system becomes involved to continue the process and sentencing reform places the offender into a more intensive program to continue the process of reformation. The next step in the process will be prison reform and how that will continue the goal of reforming the offender.

Chapter Four

Prison Reform

As explained in the last chapter on sentence reform, prison reform should continue the elimination of the notion of punishment and change its goal to reformation of the offender. In affecting this change, the term "prison" must also be changed to reflect this goal. A better term might be "reformation academy" or "reformation facility" for this denotes that the purpose would be to assist the offender in his process of improvement to result in a person who desires a better way of life than what he had prior to conviction.

Just as in police reform, prison or academy personnel must also be reformed and improved. There must be higher levels of requirements to be hired as correctional officers or better labeled "academy officers". College degrees must be required in fields such as criminal justice, social work, psychology, special designations as to drug/alcohol addiction, educational field, and other fields in order that the officers may assist the offender in his process of improvement. Just as in police hiring requirements, these officers must be vetted for any and all prejudices, biases, violent tendencies, and prior poor employment record as well as prior criminal record. Once hired, the

officer would undergo intensive training geared towards the reformation process of the offender with the emphasis on assistance rather than punishment. They would also be educated
in all the various programs available in the facility so that they
would be able to properly assist the offender in being or to assist when failures occur. The officers would be regarded as an
aid or help by the offender instead of an officer ready to punish at the slightest violation of any rule. Nevertheless, when
rules are violated, officers would have been trained to effec-
tively guide the offender in learning proper behavior in various
circumstances instead of administering types of punishment,
such as solitary confinement, removal from a job or course, or
the participation of a disciplinary course. However, with the
programs that each offender would be enrolled in at the time
of sentencing, the offender would constantly be occupied and
engaged in his studies and work so that simple violations of
academy rules would decrease. Most violations would be a failure in progressing through the program and the solution would
be to repeat the failed section until a high level of success is
achieved.

Other personnel working in the academy would be the medical staff, which would comprise doctors, nurses, psychological, psychiatric, educational, and the vocational personnel. All
these staff personnel would be full time, including a night
staff, so that any medical or psychological issues could be addressed as soon as they arise. Medical and psychological care
of the offender would be of the highest degree of excellence.
There should also be a spiritual staff of various denominations
that would provide not only religious services but also spiritual counseling and support. Most important would be an evaluation committee for the purpose of constant monitoring and
testing of the offender as he progresses through his program.

The programs that would be available to the offender would
depend upon the result of the sentencing hearing. As previ-

ously mentioned, judges would be trained in all programs available and would hear testimony from program directors as to which program would be best for each individual offender. Furthermore, the offender would have an input into which direction he desires to pursue, whether vocational or educational, and if any spiritual counseling is requested. The most common program would be drug/alcohol treatment, such as the 12-step program, along with psychological counseling as well as psychiatric treatment. Also, obtaining a GED would be required for all offenders if they were not able to obtain a high school diploma on the outside. Various college courses would be available, such as all the required subjects prior to taking courses in one's major. This would prepare the offender to continue his college studies if so, desired once released with the ability to obtain student loans. Jobs within the facility would be only on a part-time basis, for participation in other programs would take precedent and would take up most of the offender's time and effort. Vocational programs would consist of acquiring specific job skills such as plumbing, electrical, carpentry, bricklaying, HVAC repair and installation, barber training, computer science, web design, culinary studies, landscaping, and other skills that would prepare the offender for success on the outside. From the requirement of a GED, the offender would be required to participate in either group counseling or one-on-one intensive counseling. Many arrive with issues such as anger management and resolution techniques that need to be confronted and dealt with prior to moving on within their program that can result in a higher chance of success. With all that I have explained thus far, it can be easy to understand why an offender's sentence should be an indeterminate one, because to proceed through an individualized program with a high level of success will take many years. To have a definite term would only result in failure because there would be a great possibility that the offender would not have successfully completed the full range of courses in his program by his release date. For the offender convicted of lesser crimes, the sentence may be for a specific amount of time or for an indeterminate time depending upon the program he would be placed and the amount of time it would take for its successful completion.

At first glance, an assumption may be made that the sentence and prison reforms I have explained would make an offender want to go to prison, for he would receive benefits that he probably would not be able to receive if left on the outside. However, could the offender obtain those benefits, such as vocational training, higher education, drug/alcohol treatment and the like on the outside without some type of supervision or mandatory requirement? It would be difficult to accomplish, though maybe not impossible, because a person living in high crime communities does not have the same opportunities that will be provided through these prison programs. The influence and effects of this type of environment poses as a distraction and would hinder any efforts to achieve a more normal and law-abiding life style. To have such programs as I have advocated goes to the meaning of reforming the offender by placing him in a better position than prior to his conviction. This will give the offender a better opportunity for a successful life instead of doing what we have been doing for decades by releasing an offender without having accomplished any job skills or educational improvement, or without the proper assistance dealing with drug/alcohol addiction and without any other necessary support whether psychological or otherwise. This only results in offenders going through the revolving door of a failed criminal justice system.

Another area of reform is the procedure by which an inmate brings a cause of action against prison staff for brutality, medical errors or neglect, and inmate infractions. Today, an inmate is not afforded an attorney and the hearings are administratively done in-house. An inmate may not bring an action to the courts unless he has exhausted all his administrative remedies. The process seems to be against the inmate from the beginning, whereby the inmate is already deemed guilty simply because of his inmate status. These procedures need to be reformed so that an inmate may have legal representation and be conducted by an independent agency and tribunal, such as the oversight committee that is explained in my final chapter. This prevents any bias or favoritism on the part of the prison authorities conducting the administrative hearings.

From the beginning, through the bail program and up to prison reform, it is now easier to understand how all these parts of the criminal justice system must work together for the reformation of the offender. It begins at the bail stage, where the offender is provided with programs to assist him, whether guilty or not, to begin his road to a normal law-abiding life. Then, at the sentencing phase, the offender is intensely evaluated to determine the proper program that will aid him in achieving that life style with even his input in the program. After successfully progressing through and completing his program with constant monitoring and evaluations, he now arrives at being evaluated for parole. The next chapter will deal with parole reform and how parole will play a vital role in the continuation of the offender's reformation, but more importantly, his re-acclimation to society.

Chapter Five

Parole Reform

Today's system of Parole must be reformed to reflect assistance and support instead of surveillance and punishment. Many of my clients have expressed a fear when paroled because it is common practice to revoke one's parole solely based upon a parole violation that is not a crime. To live with such fear borders upon inhumane treatment of parolees and fosters distrust of the parole system. A brief account of the history of parole is necessary to better understand the present parole system and why it fails the parolee.

From its beginning in 1811, an inmate could be released only by a pardon by the governor. Then, in 1894, Maryland became the second state after Massachusetts to use probation as a correctional remedy. Around 1900, many states adopted this system where a court handed down a sentence with minimum and maximum terms and after the minimum term was completed, a board would review the inmate's record to determine if he could be released on parole. In 1914, an Advisory Board was created to supervise released inmates and in 1922 it was replaced by the Parole Commission. In the early years, parolees were supervised by volunteer guardians where by the parolee had to report monthly to the guardian, and back in those times prison sentences were either flat or determinate amounts of time. The guardian was required to submit a report documenting the parolee's behavior in the community. Prisons then became overcrowded, so governors were forced to issue mass pardons. Back in England in 1840, flat sentences were eliminated and a "mark system" was created whereby an inmate could receive early parole based on good behavior. The feeling was that early release should be related to the rehabilitation of the prisoner. By 1901, twenty states had established a parole system, and by 1944, every jurisdiction in the United States had some form of parole release and indeterminate sentences. As the parole system developed, by 1960, community supervision officers had the duty of "changing" the parolee to prevent future crime. These officers possessed great discretion and power to coerce whatever means were necessary to rehabilitate the parolee. Unfortunately, I believe this is where the parole system as well as the entire criminal justice system went astray. Isn't it the responsibility of the prison system to rehabilitate the offender? Shouldn't the inmate have been fully rehabilitated by the time he was released from prison? Apparently, the parole system was created to continue the rehabilitation process which should have already been accomplished by the prison system. This is proof that the entire criminal justice system was failing, or at the very least had the wrong concept back in its early stages. The rehabilitation or the reformation of the offender begins much earlier than in the prison. The prison system should continue the reformation in such a way that when an inmate is released on parole, the process of reformation is completed and the process of acclimating and assisting the parolee back into society begins.

A brief account of the present parole system is necessary, to fully understand the thoughts and recommendations I advocate. When an inmate is eligible for parole, he goes through a procedure that is onerous and may even be considered unfair and possibly a violation of his due process rights. The first step is that a risk assessment and a psychological evaluation is performed which can take from several months to almost a year or more in some cases. The first hearing is a closed hearing where only two parole commissioners are present, and even though the inmate may have an attorney present, the attorney is considered only an observer. It may be an open hearing if the victim of the crime agrees to be present at the hearing. The inmate never receives the results of the risk assessment and psychological evaluation, nor do the two commissioners share those reports with the inmate. The decision to grant or deny parole is then made. If parole is denied, the inmate will have a rehearing, however he is not present and will receive only a yes or no decision without any other information as to what the commissioners based their decision upon. If parole is granted, then in Maryland, the case would go before the governor if the inmate had a life sentence. The governor then has 180 days to make his decision, and the inmate is notified of either a rejection or an approval, but no explanations were given for a rejection. Unfortunately, if rejected, the inmate does not receive any recommendations as to what he needs to do to receive an approval the next time around. As mentioned earlier, the governor has been removed from the parole decision by the recent passage of Bill 202 which was vetoed by the Governor, but then overridden by the Legislature. The only two states that now have the governor involved are Hawaii and Arkansas. If after the first hearing the inmate is granted parole and is not a lifer, the next step is an En Banc closed Review where the decision goes to the entire parole commission. There is no hearing nor notice to the inmate of the review. The decision whether to grant or deny parole must have a majority vote. If denied at this stage, the inmate does have a rehearing, but again, the decision is a simple yes or no. This entire procedure could take months if not years to complete. There is no transparency as to the decision nor what it was based upon. The inmate can testify only at his first hearing, and obtaining an approval at a rehearing is difficult if the inmate fails to introduce new evidence to prove he has been rehabilitated and deserves parole approval.

To reform this part of the parole system will take full understanding of how the present system violates the rights of the inmate. Reform should be in how the parole hearings are conducted with the input of the inmate in mind. Parole hearings should be open hearings just like most court hearings are conducted. The victim should be allowed to be present along with an attorney representing the inmate with full rights of representation as in a court trial, including the right of cross examination, and to present witness testimony when necessary. If the inmate cannot afford a private attorney, he should be provided an attorney through the public defender's office. The first hearing should be a hearing before the entire parole commission in order to guarantee a speedy hearing/trial pursuant to the Constitution, for parole hearings must be considered on the same level as a trial or any other criminal/civil proceeding where the presence of the inmate is required and all his rights guaranteed. The original first hearing before two commissioners should be eliminated in order to provide a speedy process. Furthermore, the risk assessment and psychological report must be provided to the inmate and his attorney prior to the hearing for adequate time for full preparation. The decision to grant or deny parole should be made within a reasonable time so as not to further delay the process. If the inmate is granted parole, the decision should be a final one, and the governor should not be involved in the decision-making process for it tends to be more of a political decision than a fair one based upon the findings of the hearing. If parole is denied, then full detailed reasons must be given in writing along with recommendations as to what the inmate must further accomplish in order to obtain an approval at his next hearing. Also, a date for the next rehearing must be scheduled at that time along with notice of inmate's right to appeal the decision.

Another aspect of parole reform would be to expand the opportunities for release. As mentioned in the chapter on sentencing reform, cases before the Supreme Court and high State courts have confirmed the maturity issues that juvenile inmates experience. Specifically, it has been proven that a great deal of development and maturity occur between the ages of 17 through 25 and even beyond. It is this maturation process that must be taken into serious consideration in deciding if an inmate who entered prison as a juvenile, but is now an adult, should be released. In making this decision, the parole and courts must examine all that this particular type of inmate has accomplished during his stay in prison. As previously explained in the chapters on Sentencing and Prison reform, the specific program this inmate was placed into by the court and his successful progress and evaluations should play a major role in his release. This is my meaning of how all the parts of the criminal justice system must work together and be interdependent for the goal of reforming the offender. Another area for release would be for medical reasons with the same consideration of the inmate's progress through his individual program and the results of his risk assessment. Several of my clients have mentioned to me how they would hate to die in prison and how important it would be to have family around during that difficult time. Another area which has been debated for years has been the geriatric prison population. Release can be considered for inmates who have served long periods in prison, at least 50 years of age, and successful progress in his program. It has been documented that recidivism rates decline after a certain age of maturity such as in the 50s, 60s, and beyond. The last area to be considered would be not to hold an inmate after his eligibility period. This can be considered radical, however, given my prior explanation of the individual programs inmates would be required to participate in and accomplish along with the elimination of life sentences, this eligibility period would not exist. There would not be any eligibility issue, for an inmate would have to successfully complete the program before he could be considered for parole. In reality, this would be the inmate's eligibility requirement, though indefinite.

Another area of parole reform is the period after an inmate is released from prison. Today, parolees are released under certain prescribed conditions such as refraining from drugs and alcohol, no association with other offenders, obtaining and retaining employment, attending alcohol/drug treatment, meeting with an assigned parole officer monthly, and abiding by all laws and regulations. Some conditions are more specific depending on the crime committed. Unfortunately, many parolees find themselves back in prison living out the remainder of their term based on a simple violation not considered a crime. Reform should be a shifting away from law and order to assistance and acclimation into society. When an offender is released from prison, he would have successfully completed his program, which would include counseling, drug/alcohol treatment, vocational, and educational programs as I explained in the preceding chapters. With the reform of sentences and prisons, the offender is better equipped to be a success on the outside. Parole then would continue the process by helping the parolee with acquiring further job skills if necessary, continuing with drug/alcohol treatment and mental health treatment, along with seeking employment or continuing in a field of college studies. The parolee would also have housing assistance, whether it would be rental or ownership and would be provided with help in setting up bank accounts, the purchase of cell phones, driver's licenses, improving computer skills, and other necessities of life. There would be constant supervision, not to detect for any violations, but to assist the parolee in acclimating to the pressures of society. The parole agent's focus would be on assistance and support instead of focusing on infractions. In order to provide for this level of assistance, the parole officer would be specially trained in all these skills along with meeting stringent hiring requirements similar to the police. The actual parole term should also be an indeterminate one for each parolee progresses at his own pace. Once the parole agent and parolee feel that he is ready to be released from parole, a simple hearing before the parole commission would take place. The parolee would have the right to an attorney and be able to bring forth expert witnesses, such as an employer, to testify as to the parolee's ability to lead a successful and law-abiding life.

In order for a parolee to achieve this level of success, it is evident that all the parts of the criminal justice system from the police up and through parole must work together to result in the reformation of the offender. Without a simultaneous reformation of all the parts of the criminal justice system, along with respect, dignity, understanding, and tolerance for an offender, recidivism, mass incarceration, and suffering will continue.

Chapter Six

Corruption/ Oversight, Racism, and Community Improvement

Corruption/Oversight

Corruption can be found in any industry, business, and unfortunately in government agencies and has existed almost since the dawn of time. Since we live in an imperfect world with imperfect humans, corruption will always exist. Nevertheless, corruption within the criminal justice system should not be tolerated and should be prevented as much as possible because the system deals with a person's liberty, interest, and constitutional rights. Corruption in the criminal justice system is predominately seen in unethical and illegal actions on the part of the police, attorneys, prosecutors, judges, correctional and parole personnel. It can involve actions such as police knowingly failing to conduct proper investigations to hide the truth, illegal search, seizures, and arrests, prosecutors failing to provide exculpatory evidence, tampering with court documents such as transcripts, and other actions that will result in wrongful convictions. The way to eradicate or decrease the incidents of corruption is through the establishment of an oversight committee that operates within the criminal justice system, but is a separate independent agency consisting of attorneys and other professionals. Such a committee has been included in Senate Bill 600 in Maryland that will function under the Office of the Attorney General so that it will have the power to issue subpoenas, convene grand juries, and investigate police misconduct. It will increase oversight and uniformity of investigations of civilian deaths involving police by creating an independent investigative unit. However, I believe this committee should not be tied to any part of the criminal justice system such as the police, courts, prisons, or parole and should be for the entire system, not just for police misconduct. It must be an independent agency to avoid bias or favoritism of any type. The purpose of oversight would be to perform constant surveillance in a criminal case from start to finish in order that investigations and actions be brought immediately upon occurrence or after a trial is completed for any illegal, unethical, or misconduct of any kind. Once a person is arrested and entered into the system, an oversight agent is appointed to the case and follows the offender as he progresses through the system to detect any corruption, wrong doing, illegality, or unethical actions on the part of the police, bail authority, courts, attorneys, prosecutors, prison authorities and staff, and parole. If any wrong doing is detected, immediate investigation should be done and an action brought by the agent to a separate tribunal to resolve the issue instead of having these issues brought up years later. This would also involve actions brought by inmates against prison staff, as discussed in my previous chapter on prison reform. The oversight would continue up and through parole to detect any wrong doing and complaints from the offender. It took almost one year to find Officer Chauvin guilty of the murder of George Floyd and 13 months for the Justice Department to open a civil investigation into the Louisville Police Department for the shooting death of Breonna Taylor. Of course, one must take into consideration the change in the administration for these cases. With oversight, the time to open investigations and bring actions would be seriously decreased. Without oversight, any unethical, illegal, or corrupt actions would go undetected for years and in the meantime an offender who may be innocent is pronounced guilty, wrongful killing of unarmed black/brown people along with the suffering of their families, and mass incarceration would continue. What I have advocated here may not be perfect or functional, however its purpose is to begin discussions and dialogues among professionals and legislatures to think outside of the box to find the solutions to our failing system.

Racism

Just like corruption, racism has existed for centuries targeted at cultures different from ourselves. Unfortunately, racism continues to this day and seems to have become stronger in the recent years. One can look back throughout the histories of different countries to study how racism and prejudices developed, but racism exists in our hearts and minds, not in just some history story of days gone by. So much has happened over these last few years: the pandemic, the shooting and killing of young black unarmed men and teenagers by police, the mass shooting of innocent adults and children whether in schools, places of worship, work places, or social gatherings, the hatred and violence perpetrated upon the oriental and Jewish race, the assault on our Capitol Building to stop democracy from moving forward, the development of extremist positions, and the intense resurgence of white supremacy, have brought the need for reform to a head. Many demonstrations have taken place to express the frustration and desperation of all these occurrences and organizations such as Black Lives Matter have arisen from the ashes because Black Lives do matter. The question to be asked is, how can racism be eradicated if it is in our hearts and minds? Since colonial days the black people have fought the persecution of their race. There has been some change in the distant past such as the removal of black only water drinking fountains, the removal of bus back seats only for blacks, the first black person to enroll in a university, the first black president, Barack Obama, and the first black and interracial female vice president Kamala Harris being elected, more black people acquiring higher degrees and important positions in business, industries, the medical field, and government along with home and business ownership. Unfortunately, with all these hard-fought battles racism still rears its ugly head. The clincher is the way in which we fight against racism. It seems as if it has always been the black man's fight with only small progress being made over the countless decades. The fight should come from both black and white people along with other races. It is only by people of all colors joining in the fight, will we be able to demonstrate that one race is not better than another, for we are all children of God made in his likeness. More importantly, the voices of people not of the black race should be in unison with the black voice to stop racism throughout the world. For what does it matter who finds the cure for cancer and other diseases, the one vaccine to stop the spread and elimination of COVID throughout the world, the solution to end poverty and hunger, and the solutions to many other problems that all of us face today, as long as it is done, for we are all one human race facing all the same problems.

However, when it comes to racism in the criminal justice system, the issue becomes more prominent. Since the colonial days, the black population has been viewed as inferior in many ways and therefore easily labeled as criminal. According to the Baltimore Sun back in 2019, it was found that the proportion of Maryland black prison population is more than double the national average of 32%. More than 70% of Maryland's prison population was black in 2018, compared to 31% of the state population. That rate far surpassed the next closest states of Mississippi, South Carolina, and Georgia. Sadly, to say, I only had two white inmate clients, the remaining were black and all my clients were inmates housed in Maryland prisons. Eliminating this racial disparity is difficult simply because it involves reforms on many levels including the change in people's hearts and minds that no race is better than another. Disparity also exists between the rich and the poor as most people in prison come from a poor background. One question to ask is; does poverty breed crime? It most certain does though not all poor people engage in criminal behavior. The first area that needs reform are the communities with high crime rates. Most of those communities are poor black/brown neighborhoods and this is where community improvement begins. Those communities need to be lifted up and given numerous forms of assistance in order that the residents have opportunities for advancements whether in education, vocation, and employment. Furthermore, there must be help for drug/alcohol addiction as well as mental and medical treatment. It is only by improving these communities and all of us fighting for racial equality can we begin to rid the system of racism.

Community Improvement

As I mentioned in the previous section, communities plagued by poverty and crime need to be improved because this is where most crimes occur and spread to neighboring areas. The residents of these communities and neighborhoods lack the opportunities that more affluent communities possess. A far greater percentage of these residents fail to acquire a high school diploma much less a college degree. Schools in these neighborhoods not only need to be improved but also need to be reformed to meet the particular needs of these communities. Many children come home after school with little or no supervision at home and therefore very little assistance in the completion of homework assignments. Left unattended, children easily become involved in drugs, alcohol, gangs, and other criminal behavior. Teachers may find it difficult to assist those children in successfully attaining a level of achievement in the class curriculum making a child's progress almost impossible. Teachers with higher degrees and specialized training should be hired along with the creation and establishment of a curriculum that meets the needs of these students. After-school programs should be implemented for the children who require special assistance with the main core subjects such as math, science, and English. Teachers should be available during after school hours to assist with homework completion, difficulties students may have in certain subject matters, and other subjects that will advance students to their next level. Students who are successful in their studies would be provided with extra-curricular activities such as sports and other forms of exercise. Many parents who are single parents would welcome the additional curriculum programs because most are not available due to their working hours. There should also be drug/alcohol programs to help those students with addictions and guide them to a better way of life along with counseling and help from social workers when needed. I remember during my youth in certain towns, youth centers were created to provide various activities for the neighborhood youths such as sports, dances, games, band performances, food and drink services, and the like. These youth centers should also be re-established to provide healthy activities supervised by social workers, police, and other professionals during non-school hours. By improving these schools and providing these various services we may be able to place these children on the same level as those from more affluent neighborhoods. This in turn will draw the children away from a life of crime and steer them towards a more successful and rewarding life style instilling in them worthwhile goals in order to achieve a better way of life.

Not only should there be assistance for the children in these communities but also the adults for they face some of the same problems. With the improvement of the schools, there will be a greater percentage of the students obtaining their high school diploma. However, there should be GED classes held at those schools for the adults who failed to achieve that educational level. Along with GED classes there should be vocational training for all types of skilled labor such as plumbers, electricians, carpenters, bricklayers, welders, construction, mechanics, barbers, beauticians, seamstresses, short-order cooks, and trades in other industries. After completing any of the vocational programs, there should be employment services to assist a resident in writing resumes, filling out job applications, and preparing for interviews along with instructions on proper interview attire. There should also be within the high schools assistance with applying for college and financial aid for both graduating seniors and adults obtaining their GED. Also, within these communities should be child day care centers which are affordable and offer extended hours to assist those parents who need the help due to their work schedule. There should also be within these communities drug/alcohol treatment programs for adults and well as mental and medical health centers. As stated in my chapter on police reform, the police who are assigned to these communities would be working directly with all these programs and be involved with the program directors in order to not only become part of the community but also be of assistance in guiding the residents to a better way of life. Regular town hall meetings would be the norm where there would be participation of the police, psychologists, social workers, drug/alcohol specialists, and all the program directors in order that there would constant open dialogue with the residents to address any problems that arise. This will foster the trust that is needed among the residents, police, and other professionals working in those communities. Social workers and psychologists would also be available within these communities such as the Crisis Intervention Unit that is in effect in San Francesco which I mentioned earlier in the chapter on police reform. Reforming the criminal justice system is not enough, we need to lift up these hard-hit communities by injecting these specialized services that will result in a healthier, safer, more law abiding, and prosperous life. When we address and solve communities with high crime rates it also has a positive effect the criminal justice system.

Chapter Seven

My Final Thoughts

Throughout all the chapters of this book, I have advocated for many reforms and changes that some people may disagree with, find unacceptable, lack substance, or feel that those reforms would be too costly and maybe fail to produce the desired results. Also, being a criminal defense attorney, others may feel my opinions and ideas may favor the offender. However, by favoring the offender, his needs become a priority, and the true reformation of the system and the offender may be achieved. Some of my recommendations may not operate according to plan given other factors and situations involved, along with my limited knowledge and expertise of more difficult and complex issues in reforming the system. Also, I do not have knowledge of budgetary issues, however simple common sense will cause one to conclude that if a roof is about to collapse, one must expend monetary funds to replace the roof. To allow a roof to deteriorate would only lead to further damage which could be irreparable. This analogy also pertains to reforming the criminal justice system. For if we continue on our present path, future harm may be permanent to the point that a solution may not be possible. What has been brought to my attention is whether the system as a whole should be completely dismantled past its foundation and rebuilt anew. For how can we continue to retain ineffective, unethical, and even illegal procedures and laws that fail to meet our needs, corrupt police and other criminal justice authorities, but expect to attain the necessary and dire reform that is required? All aspects of the criminal justice system must be examined to determine if some laws, procedures, and other aspects need to be retained, changed, or totally eliminated. Such an undertaking seems overwhelming, but it must be seriously considered. My recommendations are not to be strictly construed, but instead carefully reflected upon and weighed as possible ideas that will lead to the actual reform needed. Many times, we have heard that the definition of insanity is doing the same thing but expecting different results. One way to avoid this insanity is to think outside of the box because it produces different and exciting possibilities that may affect change in ways unexpected. The criminal justice system has been broken for so long that we have lost track of time and the reforms that have taken place have only made a small impact. Even the recently passed legislation such as compensation for the wrongfully convicted, removal of the governor for parole decisions for lifers, recent police reform, the expansion of expungement for low level offenses, and the elimination of life sentences without parole for juveniles are signs of progress. However, all this is not enough to fully reform the system so that the offender, the sentences, procedures, other agencies of the system, and communities are drastically changed and improved to reflect the new notion of reform instead of the notion of punishment. To continue to allow the system to function in its present state only produces more suffering and fails to aid, support, and lift up the offender to become a better person. It is past the time for reform for it should have occurred many decades ago. Therefore, we must act now to right all the wrongs that have been committed by the system and to create a criminal justice system that is just and fair for all.

When the police were created in the colonial days, its purpose was to capture escaped slaves. From that time on, the Negro population has been persecuted simply because they were considered inferior and of a criminal evil nature. Unfortunately, this attitude continues to the present day. Even though slavery has been abolished, the invisible shackles of slavery still exist in the minds of some people. The evidence is found in the fact that most of the prison population is black along with the police killing of young unarmed black men. One can say that the system works as it was meant to work, but today those escaped slaves are now free young black men many of whom continue to be persecuted, harassed, wrongfully arrested and convicted, and killed simply because of racial hatred. Yes, many are guilty and have been convicted of the crimes they have committed, but the question that needs to be asked is why does the black race make up the higher percentage of the prison population and why does the system continue in its persecution of the black people? This has even been labeled not only as a violation of Constitutional rights but also a violation of civil and even human rights. Once these questions are truthfully answered will we be able to reform the system into one that aids and supports rather than harasses and punishes.

The Declaration of Independence claims that all men are created equal and that they are endowed by their Creator with certain unalienable rights, that among these are Life, Liberty, and the pursuit of happiness. This must include all races, for God, our Creator, has created us all. I can recall back in my college days when I studied criminal justice and how broken the system was and in need of reform. This was back in the mid-70's and now approximately fifty years have passed and we are still continuing to speak about reform. The only difference is that things have only gotten worse even though some small progress has been made, but not enough. When I advocate for the elimination of all drug crimes and the decrease of life sentences, it produces fear because people may conclude that criminals would be released into our communities continuing to commit crime instead of serving out their long prison sentences. The reason behind mass incarceration is not only to punish the criminals but also to keep them in prison for as long as possible for "public safety" reasons. However, with all the reforms I have stated, the offender would be given a realistic opportunity to become a law-abiding citizen ready and able to lead a productive life outside of the prison walls. It has even been mentioned that there is even a fear that the black race would eventually dominate and rule the other races. This fear has existed since the beginning and is baseless because all people whether black, white, Hispanic, or other color, desire the same thing-the chance at living a good, safe, healthy, and productive life that offers peace, financial security, prosperity, and the right to raise a family in safety, follow their religious beliefs and with opportunities available for all. I believe that it is fear and hatred that have prevented the deep reform of the system and only through their elimination will we be able to change the system to a new and more effective one. In order to rid our Country of racism, white people must fight alongside the black population to produce a system that lifts up the black race as well as other minority races so that all men, whether black, white, or other races, can attain what the Declaration of Independence Advocates-Life, Liberty, and the pursuit of happiness.

Today there is much use of the word "systemic" when speaking of racism. We need to use this word when speaking of reform in that it should be not only relating to race but also to the thoroughness of the reform of the entire criminal justice system. Since the Chauvin verdict, police reform has been in the news and in the legislative process in many states. This is long overdue, however reforming the police is not enough. There is very little mention of bail reform much less any of the other reforms I have advocated throughout this book. Systematic reform should encompass the entire criminal justice system, not just the police. Reforming only one part of the system would cause systematic failure of the entire system because where one-part results in success, the other parts, which are not reformed, will destroy that success. When all the parts of the system: police, bail, sentence, prison, and parole are reformed systematically so that all these parts work together and become interdependent with the goal of reforming the offender, then will we reduce recidivism and mass incarceration.

Today much is being said about the erosion of our democracy. In the preamble of the Constitution the first three words are "We the People,… " And in Abraham Lincoln's Gettysburg Address he stated that the "Government of the people, by the people, for the people, shall not perish from the earth." For what is the meaning of democracy but a government in which the supreme power is vested in the people and exercised by them through periodically held free elections. Since it is claimed that our democracy is being eroded, then what is to happen with the reformation of the criminal justice system and is there a correlation between the two? Unfortunately, this erosion has been occurring since the beginning of our Country and has gone unnoticed and even unacknowledged, but looking back on the history of Memorial Day, the erosion of our democracy has been occurring since the Colonial times. Memorial Day was first called Decoration Day immediately following the end of the Civil War. In the later part of the War, captured Union soldiers were housed at the transformed Washington Race Course and Jockey Club in Charleston, South Carolina. Many died by disease and exposure and were buried in mass graves. After Charleston fell, the Confederate troops left the city and the only ones remaining were the ones freed from enslavement. All the bodies buried in the mass graves were exhumed and re-interred in a new cemetery. Then on May 1, 1865 a crowd of 10,000, which were mostly freed slaves, held a parade to memorialize the fallen soldiers. This marked the earliest Memorial Day on record, and it was clear that Decoration Day was organized by freed slaves. However, once Charleston was rebuilt in the 1880s, the city's white residents had little interest in remembering the real story that it was the freed slaves that instituted Memorial Day. This is evidence that even though the slaves were free, racism and the suppression of the black people still existed and continued resulting in the beginning of the erosion of our democracy. At that time blacks, women, and other minority races did not have the right to vote immediately after the Civil War. One can see that the erosion of our democracy began in our early American history. The black race has been suppressed throughout our history in many various ways. Though they were freed slaves, the history stories reveal the reality that the black race was never really free. The black people obtained the right to vote years later, but this right is now again being suppressed. Today, a number of States have passed restrictive voting legislation that results in the suppression of the black vote along with the votes of other minority races. With this suppression comes the control of elections resulting in further racism and the real possibility of the rise and dominance of white supremacist and extremist ideologies. The reformation of the criminal justice system mainly lies in the legislative process and the voice of the people on Election Day. If the voice of the people is suppressed, then the reform that is direly needed may not occur. All the reforms I have advocated may fall on deaf ears because the legislature that may be in control may continue the racism, suppression, and suffering that has been happening since the beginning. Not only is the erosion happening today, but has gone unnoticed and unacknowledged since the beginning of our Country. I find this to be a frightening thought because what is to become of our Country if democracy is totally eradicated and what type of government will be in control? In order to accomplish solid reform, we must first address the direction and strength of our democracy to ensure that our Country is fair and just for all people, for America is a country of immigrants and we must fight against the racism and prejudices that keep us from achieving what our Declaration of Independence and the Constitution declare.

In the Chauvin trial, one of the prosecutors stated that George Floyd did not die of a large heart, but instead died of Chauvin's small heart. As I mentioned earlier, racism is in our hearts and minds and it is our hearts that first need reform. It is our hearts that need to be enlarged with the care and love for our fellow man no matter what race, creed, sex, or age and no matter what crime that was committed for most offenders, if given the proper opportunity to reform and succeed in life, the fear some people hold in their hearts and minds of criminals may vanish. We must all make a commitment to excellence in reforming the criminal justice system. That commitment is a promise to strive now and in the future for a level of excellence in how we reform the system, the offender, and the communities they reside. Our Country is still a young nation, but the time is now to grow and mature into a Country that lifts up the down trodden, treats drug usage as an illness instead of a crime, show an intolerance for corruption and unethical behavior, respect for the rule of law, love and respect for our fellow man no matter what race, whether criminal or otherwise, and a sincere desire for all men to become the best they can be in their pursuit of happiness.

About the Author

I was born and raised in Washington, D.C. My parents immigrated from Italy back in the late 1940's and early 1950's via Argentina. After coming to America, they settled in Washington, D.C. where my father had his business as a shoe cobbler. I obtained my undergraduate Degree in the Administration of Justice from the American University and my J.D. Degree at the Howard University School of Law. I practiced law in the State of Maryland for many years mainly concentrating on criminal law until my last five to six years when I only practiced in post-conviction relief and appeals from those cases. While I worked for several firms, most of my work was as a solo practitioner until I retired at the end of 2020 with a sudden need to write this book. Working with my clients who are all inmates within the Maryland Penitentiary system, I was able to witness the failures of all the parts of the criminal justice system and the great injustice being served on some of those inmates. Also, through my undergraduate studies I learned how the system fails to function as it should and what ways can be taken to reform it. It is because of this and all the recent events and current calls for reform that I felt a need to put my thoughts on paper on how I feel the system should be reformed. I only hope that my ideas may be taken seriously, and that they will cause the experts to think in different ways. I have been married for forty-five years and have two sons and four lovely grandchildren all of whom love very deeply and only wish the very best in all their future endeavors. I now reside in Frederick, Maryland and enjoy spending my time reading, writing, giving free legal advice when needed, still hearing from some of my clients, time with my family, and working on my golf swing. I will be amenable and available for speaking engagements and collaborating in discussions on the topic of criminal justice reform. I can be reached by e-mail at mdc@fiorentino-lawfirm.com.

CPSIA information can be obtained
at www.ICGtesting.com
Printed in the USA
BVHW050928230921
617399BV00017BA/469